A STUDY
ON
AWARENESS AND BEHAVIOUR OF
INDIVIDUAL INVESTORS
TOWARDS MUTUAL FUND

:: Author ::

Dr. Hukamram Pawar

PUBLISHED BY

Hemchandracharya International Publishing House
HQ. At & Po. Chaveli., Ta- Chansma,
Dist- Patan, North Gujarat, India, Asia.
www.iphouseindia.com

First Publication: 1st November, 2015

Copyright: Author

(c) **Dr. Hukamram Pawar**

ISBN:- 978-1-51950-304-6

Price: Rs.800/- INDIA

$ 15 OUTSIDE INDIA

PUBLISHED BY

Hemchandracharya International Publishing House
HQ. At & Po. Chaveli., Ta- Chansma,
Dist- Patan, North Gujarat, India, Asia.
www.iphouseindia.com

1.1 PURPOSE OF DISSERTATION AND SELECTION OF TOPIC:

As a part of curriculum of M. Phil, I have to prepare dissertation on one of the subject specified by Hemchandracharya North Gujarat University Patan. I selected the topic **"A STUDY ON AWARENESS AND BEHAVIOR OF INDIVIDUAL INVESTORS TOWARDS MUTUAL FUND"** with reference to Mehsana and Patan region.

As we probably know, mutual funds have become extremely popular over the last 15 years among individual investor in India. Till 1986, the Unit Trust of India was the only mutual fund in India. Since then public sector banks and insurance companies have been allowed to set up subsidiaries to undertake mutual fund business. So State bank of India, Canara Bank, LIC, GIC, and few other public sector banks entered the mutual fund industry. In 1992, the mutual fund industry was opened to the private sector and a number of private sector mutual funds such as Birla Mutual Fund, DSP Merill Lynch Mutual fund, HDFC Mutual Fund, IDBI Principal Mutual Fund, Tata Mutual Fund, Kotak Mahindra Mutual Fund etc. are entered in Indian mutual fund industry. Day by day such mutual fund offers different type of scheme to the individual investors at present total 49 registered mutual funds with SEBI and managing nearly 1000 schemes.

As a M. Phil student I studied the growth and development of mutual fund industries in India in depth. I also studied the behavior and awareness of individual investors by collecting information personally from investors. In this study I had trying to know that what the individual investor think about investment in mutual fund, whether mutual fund satisfied the investors need and expectation. I did this work in Mehsana and Patan region urban area only. I was trying to my subject at the level best.

1.2 OBJECTIVES OF THE STUDY:

MAIN OBJECTIVES:

The main objective of this study is to understand and analyze the awareness and behavior of individual investors toward mutual funds through an individual investor's survey in Mehsana and Patan region.

SUB OBJECTIVE:

Following aspects/ points will be analyzed during the study:-

- Study of awareness and behavior of individual investors towards mutual fund

- Study of behavior of individual investors towards various investment alternatives like bank deposits, bonds, stock, real assets etc.

- To assess the savings objectives among individual investors.

- To identify the preferred savings avenue among individual investors.

- To understand the preferential feature in the savings instrument among individual investors.

- To assess Mutual fund conceptual awareness among present investors.

- To assess the fund/ scheme preference of investors.

- To evaluate fund qualities that would affect the selection of Mutual funds.

- To perceive the preferred communication mode of investors.

- To understand the fund sponsor qualities influencing the selection of MFs/Schemes.

- To identify the information sources influencing the scheme selection decision of investors.

- To identify the most popular Mutual Funds among individual investors.

- To assess the influence of personal variables on the MF conceptual awareness level of individual investors.

- To evaluate investor related services that would affect the selection of Mutual funds.

- To establish a relationship between types of investors and MF qualities that influence MF/Scheme selection

1.3 MEANING OF INDIVIDUAL INVESTORS AND REASONS FOR THEIR INVESTMENT:

An individual are those who purchase small amounts of securities for his/herself, as opposed to an institutional investors, also called retail investors or small investors

An individual who are commits his or her money to investment products with the expectation of financial return. Generally, the primary concern of investors is to minimize risk while maximizing return, as opposed to a speculator, who is willing to accept a higher level of risk in the hopes of collecting higher-than –average profits.

Individuals like I, you and we human beings invest money for various reasons. It could be that:

i.   An individual or his/her family may be earning more than what is required for monthly expenses and thus would like to keep the money in a safe place and also allow the savings to earn a return during the period.

ii. An individual may not have regular surplus but may get occasional one time surplus earnings such as annual bonus from their employer or sale of some family property. One would like to keep such money for some time, when he/she not required, in some safe place and also allow such savings to earn a return during the period.

iii. We also invest money on education of our children like our parents did. Just as individuals do organizations to make investments. For example, we might have read news items like Reliance Industries investing ₹1000 cr. For expansion of its petrochemical division.

The above examples underline the following characteristics of an 'investment' decision:

i.   It involves the commitment of funds available with us or that we would be getting in the future.

ii. The investment leads to acquisition of a plot, house or shares and debentures.

iii. The physical or financial assets we have acquired are expected to give certain benefits in the future periods.

iv. The benefit may be in the form of regular revenue over a period of time like interest or dividend or sales or appreciation after some point of time as normally happens in the case of investments in land or precious metals.

If we think broadly, an investment is a sacrifice of existing money or other resources for future benefits. Numbers of alternatives of investment are available today. We can deposit money in a bank account or purchase a long term government securities or invest in the equity shares of a company or contribute to provident fund account or buy a stock option or acquire a plot of land or invest in some other form.

When we think about investment two key aspects generally comes in our mind viz., time and risk. The sacrifice takes place now and is certain. The benefit is expected in the future and tends to be uncertain. In some investments like government securities the time factor is key factor. In other investment like stock options the risk factor is a key factor. In yet other investments like equity shares both time and risk are important factors.

Normally every investor owns a portfolio of investment. The portfolio is a combination of various financial assets like bank deposits, bonds, stocks, and so on and real assets like car, house, and so on. The portfolio may be the result of a series of disorganized decisions or may be the result of conscious and careful planning.

Our economic well-being in the long run depends significantly on how wisely or foolishly we invest.

1.4 INVESTMENT, SPECULATION GAMBLING:

It is very difficult to draw the line between investment and speculation; it is possible to broadly distinguish characteristics of an investor from those of a speculator as follows.

Investment: An investor has a relatively longer planning horizon. His holding period is generally at least one year. Investors are normally risk averse and do not willing to take more risk. In investment an investors expect moderate return and give more significance to fundamental factors and attempts a careful evolution of the prospects of the firm. Investor uses his own funds and not borrowed funds.

Speculation: In speculation a speculator has very short planning horizon his holding period may be few days to a few months. A speculator is normally willing to take high risk a speculator is known as risk taker. Normally a speculator expects for high return in exchange of high risk he born. A speculator relies more on hearsay, technical charts, and market psychology. A speculator borrowed fund more than own funds.

Gambling: Gambling is basically different form speculation and investment in the following aspects:

- Compared to investment and speculation, the result of gambling is known more quickly. The roll of dice or the turn of a card is known almost immediately.
- Rational people gamble for fun, not for income
- Gambling does not involve a bet on an economic activity. It is based on risk that is created artificially.
- Gambling crates risk without providing any commensurate economic returns.

1.5 THE INVESTMENT DECISION PROCESS:

Investment process gives us a methodology of achieving the objectives of investment. A lot of planning is required while investing our hard earned money in securities. Often investors lose money when they make investments without any planning. They make hasty investment decision when the market and economy was at its peak based on some recommendation. Some of you might have invested during secondary market boom of 1992 and primary market boom of 1994-95. Many investors of those times are yet to recover their losses. In the year 1999-2000, investors of several software stocks, both in primary market and secondary market, have lost heavily. In all these cases, the problem is lack of planning and to an extend greed. Both are not good for making a decent return on investment. A typical investment decision undergoes a five step procedure, which in turn forms the basis of the investment process. These steps are;

    i.   Determine the investment objectives and policy

    ii.   Undertake security analysis

    iii. Construct a portfolio

    iv. Review the portfolio

    v.   Evaluate the performance of the portfolio

i) Investment objectives and policy:

The investors will have to work out his investment objectives first and then evolve a policy with the amount of investible wealth at his command. An investor might say that his objectives are to have 'large money'. You will agree that this would be a wrong way of stating the objective. You would recall that the pursuit of 'large money' is not possible without the large risk of 'large loses'. The objectives should be in clear and specific terms. It can be expressed in terms of expected return or expected risk. Suppose, an investor can aim to earn 12% return against the risk-free rate of 9%. It means the investor is willing to assume some amount of risk while making investment. Alternatively, the investor can set her or his preference on risk by stating that the risk of Investment should be below market risk. Setting of investment objectives is good, many investors fail to do the same and blindly invest their money without bothering the risk associated with such investments. Investments are bound to fail if an investor ignores this point.

The next step in formulating the investment policy of an investor would be the identification of categories of financial assets he/she would be interested in. It is obvious that this in turn, would depend on the objectives, amount of wealth and the tax status of the investor. For example, a tax exempt investor with large investible wealth like pension/provident fund would invest anything but tax exempt securities unless compelled by law to do so. Some investors may entirely avoid derivatives because of high risk associated with such investments. Some investors may invest more in equities to earn higher return but use derivatives to reduce additional risk. As in consumer products, financial products also come with different colours and flavors and one has to be highly knowledgeable before selecting appropriate securities.

ii) Security Analysis:

After defining the investment objective and broadly setting the proportion of wealth to be invested under different categories, the next step is selecting individual securities under each category. For instance, if an investor sets 50% of his/her wealth to be invested in the government securities, the next question is which of the government securities that the investment should be made. It should be noted that all the government securities are not same. A long term government bond is much riskier than short term bonds. Similarly, an investment in equities requires identification of companies stocks, in which the investment can be made. Security analysis is often performed in two or three stages. The **first stage**, called **economic analysis,** would be useful to set broad investment objective. If the economy is expected to do well, investor can invest more in stock. On the other hand, if the economic slowdown is expected to continue, investor can invest less in stock and more in bond. In **second stage**, investors typically examine the industries and identify the industries, in which investment can be made. Investment need not be made any one specific industry because many of the stocks may be overpriced in a growth industry. It is better to look for three to five industries and it depends on individual's choice. The issued is an analysis of broad trends of industry and future outlook is essential to proceed further on security analysis.

At the **last step**, one has to look into the fundamentals of specific companies and find whether the stock is desirable for investment. At this stage, investors need to match the risk-return objective he/she set in the previous stage. Company specific analysis includes examination of historical financial information as well as future outlook. Using historical performance and future outlook, specifically the future cash flows are projected and discounted to present value. Through such analysis, analysts quantify the intrinsic value of the stock and compare the same with current price. It the intrinsic value is greater than the current market price the stock qualifies for investment. For instance, if investors based on his/her understanding and estimation of cash flows find the intrinsic value of Hindustan lever is ₹300 against its market price of ₹250, then the stock qualifies for investment.

Similar analysis has to be done for other socks too. Since a large number of stocks are traded in the market, it may be difficult to perform such analysis for all stocks. Normally, investors use certain conditions to reduce the number of stock, the investors would like to examine whether fits into the risk – return profile that was outlined earlier.

iii) Portfolio Construction:

In the previous stage, bonds and stocks, which fulfill certain conditions, are identified for investments. Under portfolio construction stage, the investor has to allocate the wealth to different stocks; a couple of principles guide such allocation of wealth. Investors need to appreciate that the risks of portfolio come down if the portfolio is diversified. Diversification here doesn't mean more than one stock but stocks whose future performance is not highly correlated. Further, too much diversification or too many stocks may also create problem in terms of monitoring. For example, it the investor decides to invest 10% wealth in software sector, it would be desirable to restrict the investment in two or three stock based on the amount of investment. On the other hand, if he /she invest in 20 software stocks, the portfolio will become too large and create practical problem of monitoring. While including stock in portfolio, the investor has to watch its impact on the overall portfolio return and risk and also examine whether it is consistent with the initial investment objective.

Portfolio construction is not done once for all. Since investor's savings takes place over a period of time, portfolios are also constructed over a period of time. It is a continuous exercise. Some time, timing of investment may be critical. For instance, if an investor saves ₹30,000 during the first quarter and the desired portfolio includes both bonds and stocks, the issue before the investor is whether the amount has to be used for bonds or stocks or both. It requires some further analysis at that point of time. However over the years, when the accumulated investments grow to certain level, subsequent yearly investments as proportion of total investment will become smaller and hence the timing issue will become minor decision.

iv) Portfolio Revision:

Under portfolio construction, investors are matching the risk-return characteristics of securities with the risk-return of investment objective. Under two conditions, the securities in which investment was made earlier, require liquidation and investing the amount in a new security. The risk or expected return of the security might have changed over a period of time when the business environment changes. For instance, the software sector, which was showing 100% growth between 1995-2000 have suddenly become risky after the U.S. slowdown. Many frontline companies have revised their estimated earnings growth from 100% to 40%. The stock might also become less risky but offer lower return. That is, when the risk-return characteristics of securities change, it will affect the desired risk-return characteristics of portfolio and hence calls for a revision of portfolio of stocks. Another reason for selling some of the securities in the portfolio and buying new one in its place is a change in investment objective. For instance, when you are young and have less family commitments, then your investment objectives my aim for higher return even if it amount to higher risk. You may invest more of your savings in equity stocks and derivatives. When your family grows, you might want to reduce the risk and change the investment objective. Portfolio of securities has to be revised to reflect your new investment objective. There is yet another reason for revision, which we discussed earlier. When the macro-economic condition changes, you may want to shift part of your investment from equity to debt or vice versa depending on the future economic outlook.

v) Portfolio Performance Evaluation:

The value of your investment changes over a period of time and it reflects the current market value of the securities in the portfolio. For instance, if you made some investment in Hindustan Lever 10 years back, when your first started investing, the value of HLL today is several times more than its value 10 years back. Few stocks could have resulted in a loss and it would be difficult to construct a portfolio of stocks only with winner stocks. Portfolio return reflects the net impact of positive and negative returns of individual securities in the portfolio. At the end of each period, you may like to compute the portfolio return and risk and compare the same with your investment objective as well as certain benchmark risk-return. The objective of this exercise is to evaluate the efficiency in construction and management of portfolio.

1.6 THE INVESTMENT ENVIRONMENT:

In the forgoing paragraph we discussed the basic principles of investment. Suppose an individual able to frame their investment objectives and also identified securities that are to be purchased. Now he/she need to deal with the market for the purchase and sale of securities. An understanding of the operational details of the market would be useful. Investment decision to buy or sell securities taken by individuals and institutions are carried through a set of rules and regulations. There is markets-money and capital that function subject to such rules and established procedures and are, in turn regulated by legally constituted authority. Then there are securities or financial instruments which are the objects of purchase and sale. Finally, the mechanism, which expedites transfers from one owner to another, comprises a host of intermediaries. All these elements comprise the investment environment; investors have to be fully aware of this environment for making optimal investment decisions.

Discussion in the following paragraphs provides a brief overview of the three elements of the investment environment viz., **instruments, institutions, and markets:**

i) Financial Instruments:

Financial assets or instruments can be classified in a variety of ways. We will classify them into creditorship and ownership securities on the basis of the nature of the buyer's commitment. The description will then be split into public and private issued differentiating the two major form of issuance.

Creditorship Securities:

Debt instruments furnish an evidence of indebtedness of the issuer to the buyer. Periodic payments on such instruments are generally mandatory and all of them provide for the eventual repayment at maturity of the principal amount. Securities may also be sold at a price below the eventual redemption price, the difference between the redemption price and the sale price constitution the interest. For example, a buyer of a ₹100 bond/debenture may receive an interest at 6% for one year in one of the following ways:

- He pays ₹100 at the time of investment and receives ₹106 at the end of one year, or

- He pays ₹94 at the beginning and receives ₹100 at maturity i.e. he receives 6% of ₹94 that is equal to the difference between ₹100 (redemption price) and ₹94 (issue price).

The latter arrangements are known as zero interest bonds. The interest amount in rupees measured as a percent of the par value of debt instrument is known as nominal or coupon rate of interest. For example, ₹28 payable per year on a debenture whose face/par value is ₹200 yields a coupon rate of 14% per annum.

Debt instruments can be issued by public bodies and governments and also by private business firms.

Public Debt Instruments:

Government issues debt instruments for long and short periods. They are rated the best in terms of quality and are risk-free. A common term used to designate them is "gilt-edged securities". The 182 day treasury bills issued by the Government of India are examples of short-term instruments. Government also borrows money for long –term and 11.5% loan 2009 (V issue) of government of India is an example of long-term instruments. State government and local bodies also issue series of loans and bonds. Banks, insurance, pension and provident funds, and several other organizations buy government debt instruments in compliance with their statutory obligations. Such debt instruments are usually over-subscribed. You can refer money market page on any one of the financial dailies, where you can find the list to short-term long-term securities that were bought and sold on a particular day.

Private Debt Instruments:

These are issued by private business firms, which are incorporated as companies under the Companies Act, 1956. Generally these instruments are secured by a mortgage on the fixed assets of a company. In addition to plain debt instruments, there are several variations. A very popular variety of such debentures are 'convertible' whereby either whole or a part of the par value of a debenture is convertible (either automatically or at the option of investors) on the expiry of a stipulated period after issue. The terms of conversion are stated in advance. There may be a series of conversions and price may differ from period to period.

Selected Indian companies are now raising short-term funds by issuing a debt instrument known as Commercial paper (CP). The Reserve Bank of India has issued detailed guidelines in January 1990 in this regard. They are contained in "Non-Banking Companies (Acceptance of deposits through the Commercial Paper) Directives, 1989." The eligibility for entering into the CP market is based on transparent norm, which companies themselves, can readily assess. These conditions were relaxed in April 1990.

Special Debt Instruments:

With a view to mop up resources and innovating the spectrum of debt-instruments, two new debt instruments deserve a special mention viz., Public sector undertaking(PSU) bonds (long-term) and Certificate of deposit (Short-term).

The PSU bonds are issued to the general public and financial institutions by public sector undertakings, usually with tax incentive. It is interesting to note that a large proportion of PSU bonds are privately placed with banks, their subsidiaries, and financial institutions. Certificates of Deposits (CDs) were introduced in June 1989. Commercial banks are permitted to issue CDs within a ceiling equal to 2% of their fortnightly average outstanding aggregate deposits. The maturity of 3 months at the short-end and one-year at the long –end was generally popular with investors. Interest rates for CDs are normally higher than the interest rate offered by the bank for similar maturity period deposits.

Ownership Securities:

These instruments are called 'equities' because investors who invest in them get a right to share residual profits. Equity investment may be acquired indirectly or even through a hybrid instrument known as preference shares. They are discussed in this order.

Indirect Equities:

The investors acquires special instrument of institution, who take the buy-sell decision on behalf of investors. Such institutions are **Unit Trust or Mutual Funds.** An individual who buys Unit gets a dividend from the income of the Trust/Mutual fund after meeting all expenses of management. The Units can buy from and sold to the institution at sale and repurchase prices announced from time to time (on a daily basis). Many mutual funds schemes are also listed in stock exchanges and investors can also sell and purchase the Units through secondary markets. The objectives of Trust and Mutual Funds is to use their professional expertise in portfolio constructions and pass on the benefits to the small investor who cannot repeat such performance is left alone to subscribe to equity share directly.

Direct Equities:

The investor can subscribe directly to the equity issues place on the market by the new companies or by the existing companies. If he/she is already a shareholder of an existing company, which enters the capital market for additional issue of equity shares, such an investor would get a pro rata right to subscribe, on a pre-emptive basis, to the new issue. Such offerings are known as 'rights shares'. Established companies reward their shareholders by giving them 'bonus shares'. They are given out the accumulated reserves and shareholders need not pay any cash consideration as happens in the case of 'right shares'.

Preference share:

This instrument is less popular as compare to equity and other instrument. It is neither full debt nor full equity and is, therefore, recognized as a 'hybrid security'. Such a shareholder would have certain preference over equity shareholder. They may relate to dividends, redemption, participation and conversion, etc. the most common is with regard to dividends which, when not paid for any particular year, get accumulated and no equity dividend would be payable in future until such accumulated areas of preference dividend are cleared. The dividend rate on these shares is normally less than the one on equity shares but greater than interest rate.

ii) Financial Intermediaries:

Financial intermediaries perform the intermediation function i.e., they bring the users of funds and the suppliers of funds together. Many of them issue financial claims against themselves and use cash proceeds to purchase the financial assets of others. The Unit Trust of India and other mutual funds belong to this category.

Most financial institution underwrites issue of capital by non-governmental public limited companies in addition to directly subscribing to such capital either under a public issue or under a private placement. In 1992, SEBI required all equity issues were to be underwritten fully but this requirement was withdrawn subsequently. The percentage of underwriting has come down substantially after the withdrawal of this requirement. While good issues require no underwriting, underwriters are not willing to underwrite bad issues.

The financial institutions engaged in intermediary activities include the Industrial Development Bank of India (IDBI), Industrial Finance Corporation of India (IFCI), Industrial Credit and Investment Corporation of India (ICICI), Unit Trust of India (UTI), Life Insurance Corporation (LIC), and General Insurance Corporation (GIC). Two institutions, which have broadened financial services activities in India, deserve a special mention. They are: The Credit Rating Information Services of India Ltd., (CRISIL) and other credit rating agencies, and the Stockholding Corporation of India Ltd. (SHCIL).

CRISIL, the first credit rating agency of the country, was set up jointly by ICICI, UTI, LIC, GIC, and Asian Development Bank. It started operations in January 1988 and has rated a large number of debt instruments and public deposits of companies. CRISIL ratings provide a guide to investors as to the risk of timely payment of interest and principal on a particular debt instruments and preference shares on receipt of request from a company. Ratings relate to a specific instrument and not to the company as a whole. They are based on factors like industry risk, market position and operating efficiency of the company, track record of management, planning and control system, accounting, quality and financial flexibility, profitability and financial position of the company, and its liquidity management.

The SHCIL was sponsored by IDBI, IFCI, ICICI, UTI, GIC and IRBI to introduce a book entry system for the transfer of shares and other types of scripts replacing the present system that involves voluminous paper work. The corporation commenced its operations in August 1988. Commencing its operation with UTI, SHCIL has now extended its operations to GIC, LIC mutual fund and New India Assurance Co. Ltd.

iii) Financial Markets:

Securities markets can be seen as primary and secondary. The primary market or the new market is an informal forum with national and even international boundaries. Anybody who has funds and the inclination to invest in securities would be considered a part of this market. **Individual**, trust, banks, **mutual funds**, financial institutions, pension funds, and for that matter any entity can participate in such markets. Companies enter this market with initial and subsequent issues of capital. They are required to follow the guideline prescribed by the regulating agencies like SEBI from time to time unless they are expressly exempted from doing so. A prospectus or a statement-in-lieu of prospectus is a necessary requirement because this contains all material information on the basis of which the investor would from judgment to put or not to put his money. Concealment and misrepresentations in these documents have serious legal implications including the annulment of the issue.

Some companies would use the primary market by using their 'in house' skill but most of them would employ brokers, broking and underwriting firm, issue managers, lead managers for planning and monitoring the new issue. New guidelines issued by the Securities & Exchange Board of India (SEBI), now require the compulsory appointment of a registered merchant broker as issue manager where the amount of the capital issue exceeds ₹50 lacks

The secondary markets or stock exchanges are set up under the Securities Contracts (Regulation) Act, 1956. They are known as recognized exchanges and operate within precincts those possess networks of communication, automatic information scans, and other mechanized system. Members are admitted against purchase of a membership card whose official prices vary according to the size and seniority of the exchange. Membership cards generally command high unofficial preemie because the number of members is not easily expandable. Business was earlier transacted on the trading floor within official working hours under the open bid system. Today, all exchanges in India have introduced screen based trading where the members of the exchange transact the business (purchase and sale of securities) through computer terminals. Methods of recording and settlement are laid down in advance and members are obligated to follow them. Arbitration procedures exist for the resolution of disputes. The regulatory mechanism relating to capital market has seen major changes during the last ten years. The Securities and Exchange Board of India (SEBI) is now responsible to monitor and control the stock market operations, new capital issues, working of mutual fund merchant bankers and other intermediaries. SEBI has issued separate guidelines for each of the above entities and requires all the intermediaries to register with the SEBI and periodically submit the report on their operations.

1.7 INVESMTNE ALTERNATIVES AVAILABLE IN MARKET:

An investor has a wide range of Investment avenues available in the market. Classification of various alternatives may show below.

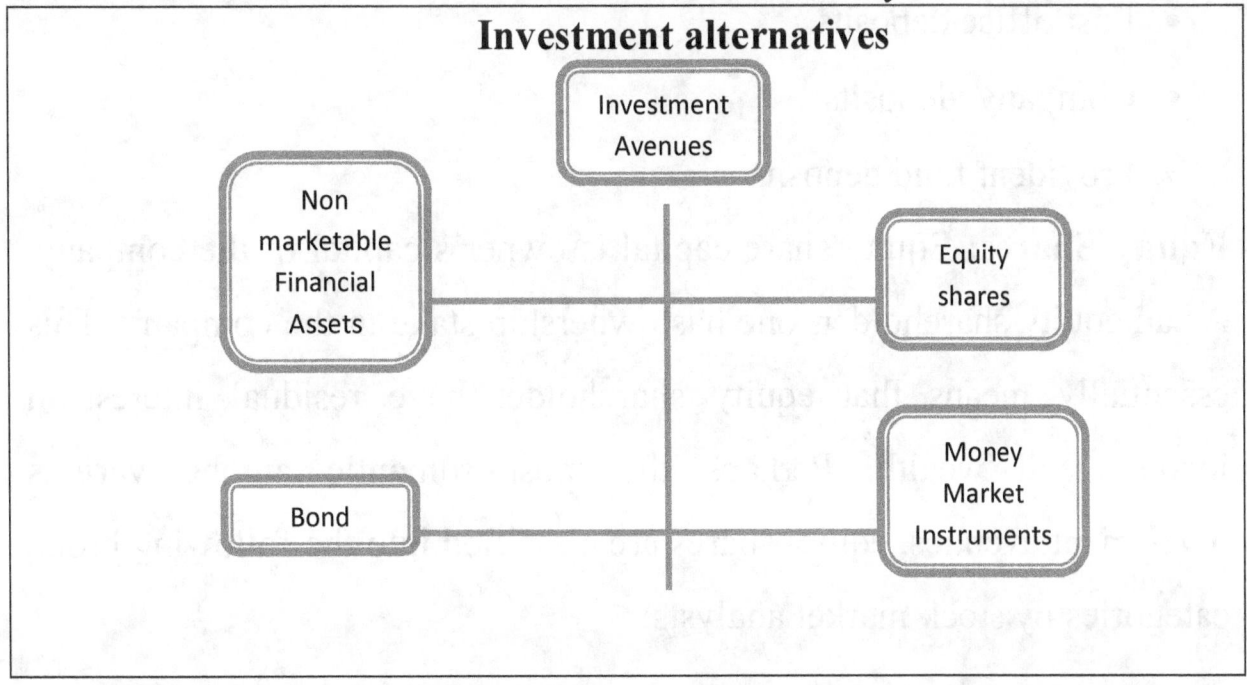

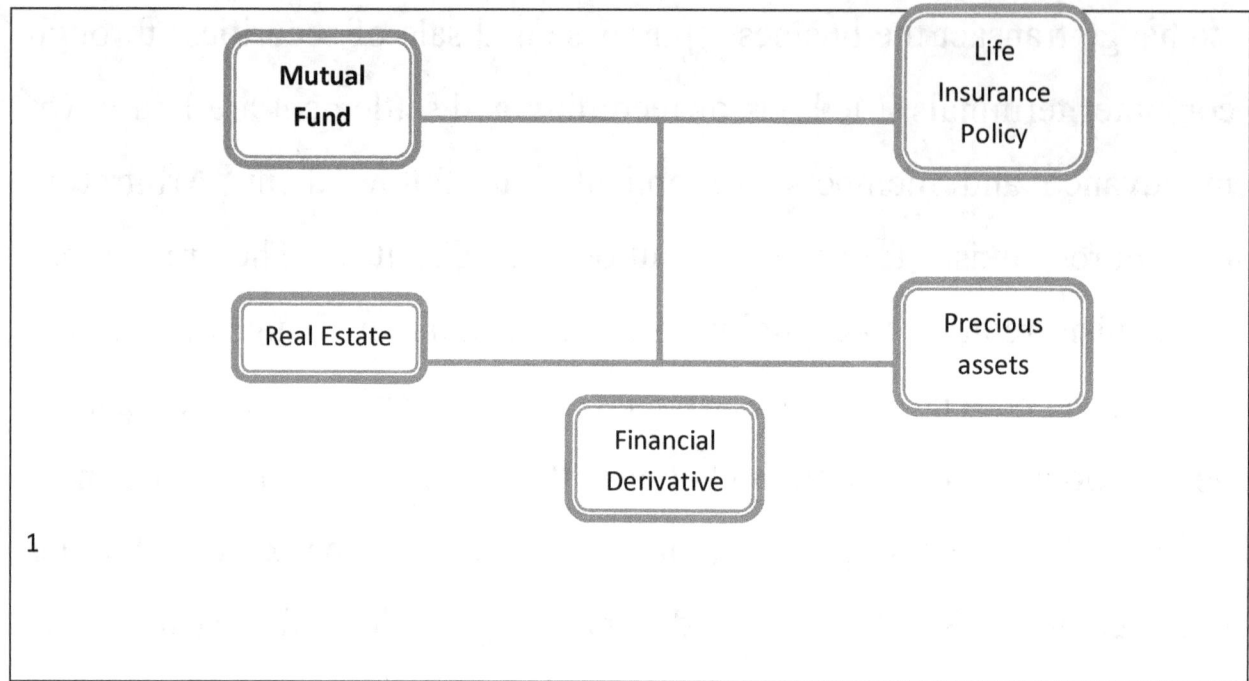

Non Marketable Financial Assets: A good portion of financial assets is represented by non marketable financial assets. They can be classified in the following broad categories.

- Band deposits
- Post office deposits
- Company deposits
- Provident fund deposits

Equity Shares: Equity share capital is owner's capital of the company. As an equity shareholder, one has ownership stake in the company. This essentially means that equity shareholder have residual interest in income and wealth. Perhaps the most romantic among various investment avenues, equity shares are classified into the following broad categories by stock market analysts:

---

[1] Chandra prasanna, *Investment analysis and portfolio management,* Tata McGraw hill publication 2008.

- Blue chip shares
- Growth shares
- Income shares
- Cyclical shares
- Speculative shares

Bonds: Bonds or debenture represent long – term debt instruments. The issuer of bond promises to pay a stipulated stream of cash flow in the form of interest. Bond may be classified into the following categories:

- Government securities
- Savings bonds
- Government agency securities
- PSU bonds
- Debentures of private sector companies
- Preference share[2]

Money Market Instruments: This kind of debt instrument having maturity period of less than one year at the time of issued. Such kinds of instruments are known as short time source of finance. The important money market instruments are:

- Treasury bills
- Commercial paper

---

[2] Preference shares are hybrid securities which have features of bonds and equity shares. For sake of simplicity, I include them under bonds.

- Certificates of deposit

Mutual Funds: Instead of directly buying equity shares and /or fixed income instruments, one can participate in various schemes floated by mutual funds which, in turn, invest in equity shares and fixed income securities. There are three broad types of mutual fund schemes:

- Equity schemes
- Debt schemes
- Balanced schemes

Life insurance[3]: In broad sense, life insurance may be viewed as an investment. Insurance premiums represent the sacrifice and the assured sum, the benefit. The important types of insurance policies in India are:

- Endowment assurance policy
- Money back policy
- Whole life policy
- Term assurance policy

Real Estate: For the bulk of the investors the most important asset in their portfolio is residential house. In addition to a residential house, the money affluent investors are likely to be interested in the following types of real estate.

---

[3]Life insurance policies are also non marketable financial assets. Given their distinctive character I have treated them as a separate category.

- Agriculture land

- Semi urban land

- Commercial property

- A resort home

- A second house

Precious Objects: Precious objects are items that are generally small in size but highly valuable in monetary terms. The important precious objects are:

- Gold and silver

- Precious stones

- Art objects

Financial Derivatives: A financial derivative is an instrument whose value is derived from the value of an underlying asset. It may be viewed as a side bet on the asset. The most important financial derivatives from the point of investors are:

- Options
- Futures

2.1 MUTUAL FUND - AN INTRODUCTION:

Mutual Fund is an important segment of the financial system. Mutual Fund is a non-fund based special type of institution which acts as an investment conduit. It is essentially a mechanism of pooling together the savings of large number of investors for collective investment with an avowed objective of attractive yield and appreciation in their value. A Mutual Fund is a financial services organization that receives money from shareholders, invests it, earns return on it, attempts to make it grow and agree to pay the share holder cash on demand for the current value of his investment. A Mutual fund offers investors a proportionate claim on portfolio assets that fluctuates in value with the value of the assets that make up the intermediaries portfolio. It is rather difficult to give a comprehensive concept of a mutual fund. What is mutual fund is better understood by the functions it performs and role it plays. It is a non depository financial intermediary. Mutual funds are mobilizer of savings, particularly from the small and household sectors, for investment for investment in stock and money markets. Mutual funds mobilize fund by selling their own share also known a units. When an investor owns a unit in mutual funds he owns a proportional share of the securities portfolio held by a mutual fund. In other words, share of a mutual fund actually represents a part share in many securities that it has purchased. Mutual fund share/unit certificate combines the convenience and satisfaction of owning shares in many industries. Thus, mutual funds are primarily investment intermediaries which pool investors' fund to acquire individual investment and pass on the return thereof to fund investors.

2.2 CONCEPT OF MUTUAL FUND:

Probably nothing can define the spirit of being 'mutual' better than this verse. And who else to understand it better than the mutual fund industry.

A Mutual Fund is a trust that pools the savings of a number of investors who share a common financial goal. The money thus collected is then invested in capital market instruments such as shares, debentures and other securities. The income earned through these investments and the capital appreciation realized is shared by its unit holders in proportion to the number of units owned by them. Thus a Mutual Fund is the most suitable investment for the common man as it offers an opportunity to invest in a diversified, professionally managed basket of securities at a relatively low cost. The flow chart on next page describes broadly the working of a mutual fund:

Some definition of Mutual funds:

- According to James L. Pierce, it is non-depository or non-banking financial intermediary which acts as an "important vehicle for bringing wealth holders and deficit units together indirectly".

- Frank Reily defines mutual funds as "financial intermediaries which bring a wide variety of securities within the reach of the most modest of investors".

- Joel Ross defines mutual fund as" taking pool of money and investing it in the securities of a wide range of companies".

- VNR dictionary of business and finance says mutual fund is "an investment fund that pools the invested funds of others and invests money market instruments, municipal bonds, or common stock".

- Thomson dictionary of banking defines a unit trust as "a method of investment by which money subscribed by many people is pooled in a fund, the investment and management of which is subject to the strict legal provision of a trust deed".

- The Securities and Exchange Board of India (Mutual Funds) Regulations, 1996 defines a mutual fund as a 'A fund established in form of a trust to raise money to through the sales of units to public or a section of the public under one or more schemes for investing in securities, including money market instruments'.

According to the above definitions, a mutual fund in India can raise sources through sales of units to the public. It can be set up in the form of Trust under the Indian Trust Act. The definition has further extended by following mutual fund to diversify their activities in the following areas:

- Portfolio management services
- Management of offshore funds
- Providing advice to offshore funds
- Management of pension or provident funds
- Management of venture capital funds

- Management of money market funds

- Management of real estate funds

Thus, mutual fund serves as a link between investor and the securities market by mobilizing savings from the investors and investing them in the securities market to generate returns.

[4]**Figure -2.1: Mutual fund operation flow chart**

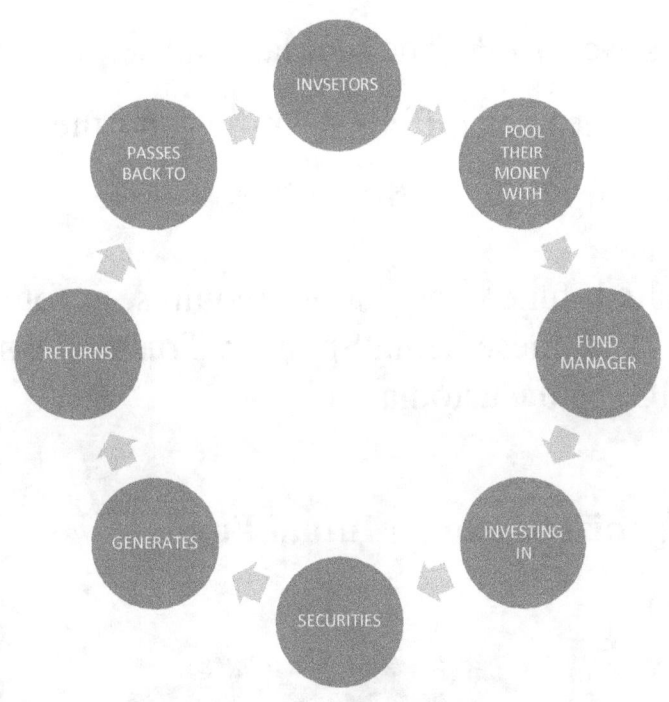

2.3 ORGANISATION OF MUTUAL FUND:

A Mutual fund can be constituted either as a corporate entity or as a trust. In India, Unit Trust of India (UTI) was set up as a corporation under an Act of parliament in 1964. SEBI regulation on

---

[4] Source: MS-44 Security Analysis and Portfolio Management (IGNOU) study material unit 16 p 30

Mutual fund requires a mutual fund be constituted in the form of a trust. The instrument of trust shall be in the form of a deed, duly registered under the provision of the Indian Registration Act, 1908 executed by the sponsor in favour of the trustees named in such an instrument. While Mutual Fund registered as trust floats schemes and collects money, the actual investment is made by a different entity call Asset Management Company (AMC). AMC is typically constituted as a company registered under Companies Act. 1956. The mutual fund set up is slightly complex because of involvement of different entities and the following diagram shows the relationship between the entities.

SEBI (Mutual fund) regulation requires a four tier system to organize mutual fund, these being Sponsor, Trustee, Assets Management Companies (AMC), and Custodian.

[5]**Figure -2.2 Organization of a Mutual Fund**

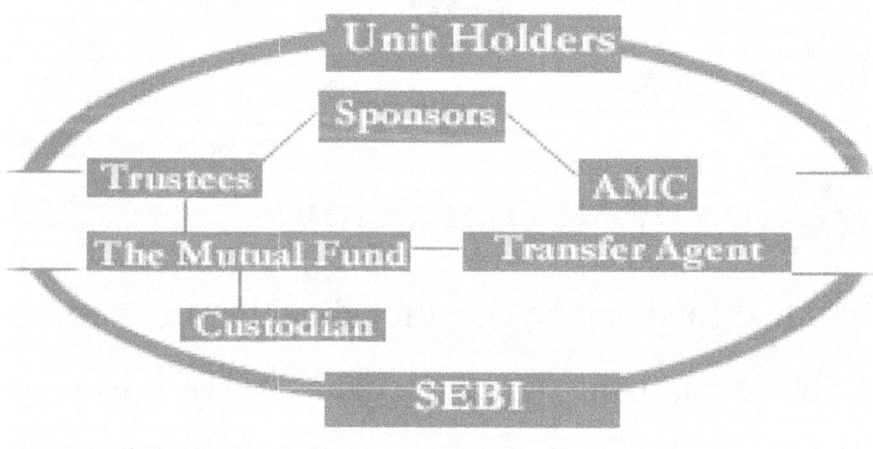

---

[5] Source: MS-44 Security Analysis and Portfolio Management (IGNOU) study material unit 16 p 31

Sponsors:

It refers to anybody corporate which initiates the launchings of a mutual fund. It is this agency which of its own, if eligible or in collaboration with other body corporate complies the formalities of establishing a mutual fund. The sponsor should have a sound track record and experience in the relevant field of financial services for a minimum period of five years. SEBI ensure that sponsors should have professional competence, financial soundness and general reputation of fairness and integrity in business transactions. Every mutual fund shall be registered under the said regulations and it is the sponsor who files an application (format is prescribed) with fee to SEBI. Sponsor is also to contribute at least 40% of the net worth of the Asset Management Company. It is the sponsors who identify and appoint the trustees and AMC. Sponsors are to submit the trust deed and draft of memorandum and Articles of Association of AMC. Once MF is registered, the sponsors technically go in background.

Trustees:

A Mutual fund is to be constituted as a Trust under Indian Trust Act, 1982 and registered under SEBI. Trustees are to look after the trust. A trustee is a person who holds the property of the mutual fund in trust for the benefit of the unit holders. A company is appointed as a trustee to manage the mutual fund with approval of SEBI. To ensure fair dealings, at least 75% of the trustees are to be independent of the sponsors. Trustees take into their custody, or under their control all the property. It is duty of the trustees to provide information to unit holders as well as to SEBI about the mutual fund schemes. Trustees are to appoint as Asset Management Company (AMC) to float the schemes. The trustees are to evolve Investment Management Agreement to be entered into with AMC. It is trustee's duty to observe and ensure that AMC is managing schemes in accordance with the trust deed. Trustees can dismiss the appointed AMC. It is the responsibility of trustees to supervise the collection of any income due to be paid to the scheme. Trustee for their services are paid trusteeship fee which is to be specified in the trust deed. Trustees are to present annual report to the investors.

Assets Management Companies:

The sponsor or the trustees appoint an AMC, also known as 'Investment Manager', to manage the affairs of the mutual fund. It is the AMC which operates all the schemes of the fund. Any AMC cannot act as a trustee of any other mutual fund. AMC can act as AMC of only one mutual fund. AMC is not permitted to undertake any business activity except activities in the nature of management and advisory services to off shore funds, pension fund, provident funds, and venture capital fund, management of insurance funds, financial consultancy fund and exchange of research on commercial basis, if these activities are not in conflict with the activities of mutual fund. It can also operate as an underwriter provided it gets registered under SEBI (Merchant Bankers) Regulation.

In the Indian context, the sponsors promote the Asset Management Company also, in which it holds a majority stake. In many cases a sponsor can hold a 100% stake in the Asset Management Company (AMC). E.g. Birla Global Finance is the sponsor of the Birla Sun Life Asset Management Company Ltd., which has floated different mutual funds schemes and also acts as an asset manager for the funds collected under the schemes.

Types of AMCs in Indian Context:

- The following are the types of AMCs we have in India
- AMCs owned by banks
- AMCs owned by financial institutions
- AMCs owned by the Indian private sector companies
- AMCs owned jointly by Indian and foreign investors.

Different AMCs Working in India are:

[6]**Table: 2.1**

	NAME OF AMC
A) BANK SPONSORED:	BOB Assets Management Company Ltd. Canbank Assets Management Services Ltd. PNB Asset Management Co. Ltd. SBI Fund Management Ltd.

---

[6] Source: Web site of AMFI www.amfiindia.com

	UTI Asset Management Company Pvt. Ltd.
B) INSTITUTIONS:	GIC Assets Management Co. Ltd. IL & FS Asset Management Co. Ltd. Jeevan Bima Sahayog Asset Management Co. Ltd.
C) PRIVATE SECTOR: **(1) INDIAN:**	Benchmark Asset Management Co. Pvt. Ltd. Escorts Asset Management Ltd. Sahara Asset Management Co. Pvt. Ltd. J.M. Capital Management Pvt. Ltd. Kotak Mahindra Asset Management Co. Ltd. Reliance Capital Asset Management Ltd. Sundram Assct Management Company Ltd.
(2) FOREIGN:	Principle Asset Management Co. Pvt. Ltd.
(3) JOINT VENTURES-PREDOMINANTLY INDIAN	Birla Sun Life Asset Management Co. Ltd. Credit Capital Asset Management Co. Ltd. DSP Merrill Lynch Fund Managers Ltd. HDFC Asset Management Co. Ltd. Tata TD Asset Management Private Ltd.

(4) JOINT VENTURES-PREDOMINANTLY FORIGN	Alliance Capital Asset Management (India) Ltd.
	Deutsche Asset Management (India) Ltd.
	HSBC Asset Management (India) Pvt. Ltd.
	ING Investment Management (India) Pvt. Ltd.
	Morgan Stanley Investment Management Pvt. Ltd.
	Prudential ICICI assets Management Co. Ltd.
	Standard Chartered Asset Management CO. Pvt. Ltd.
	Sun F & C Asset Management (India) Pvt. Ltd.
	Franklin Templeton Asset Management (India) Pvt. Ltd.

Transfer Agent:

A transfer agent is employed by a mutual fund to maintain record of shareholder accounts, calculate and disburse dividends, and prepare and mail shareholder account statements, federal income tax information, and other shareholder notices. Some transfer agents prepare and mail statements confirming shareholder transactions and account balances, and maintain customer services departments to respond to shareholder inquires. The major responsibilities include:

- Receiving and processing the application form of investors.
- Issuing of Unit/Share certificates on behalf of Mutual Fund.

- Maintain detailed records of Unit holder's transactions.

- Purchasing, selling, transferring and redeeming the Unit/Share Certificates.

- Issuing of income/dividend warrants, cheques etc.

- Creating security interest on Units/Certificates for allowing loans against them.

Custodians:

In a mutual fund depending on its size there is substantial work involved in managing the scrips bought from and sold in the market. Their safe custody and ready availability is to be ensured. SEBI requires that each mutual fund shall have a custodian who is not in any way associated with the Asset Management Company. Such custodian cannot act as sponsor or trustee of any mutual fund. Further, custodian is not permitted to act as a custodian to more than one mutual fund without the prior approval of SEBI. A custodian's main assignment is safekeeping of the securities or participation in any clearing system on behalf of the client to effect delivers of the securities. The custodian, depending on terms of agreement, also collects income/dividends on the securities. Some of the other associate assignments of custodians are;

- Ensuring delivery of scrips only on receipt of payment and payment on upon receipt of scrips.

- Regular reconciliation of assets to accounting records.

- Timely resolution on discrepancies and failures.
- Securities are properly registered or recorded.

Depending on the volume there can be co-custodians for a mutual fund. These custodians are entitled to receive custodianship fee, based on the average weekly value of net assets or sale and purchases of securities along with per certificate custody charges.

Besides the above, other players who are involved in the Mutual fund activities are as under:

- Fund Administrator
- Fund Accounting Services
- Advertiser
- Legal Advisors
- Fund officers
- Underwriter/Distributors

The basis of payment to various players for their services in organizing a Mutual Fund is given in the table given below. The SEBI regulation on mutual funds also to an extent governs the service charges and management fee. Considering the importance of mutual funds and large amount of public money being vested with such funds, the SEBI has brought out a detailed guideline. Since the mutual funds are typically promoted by an existing financial service company or leading industrial group, the SEBI regulation put various restrictions while investing the mutual funds money. It also required a kind of arm-length relationship between the sponsors or their companies and the management of the mutual fund.

Basis for Service Charges to Intermediaries Associated with Mutual Fund

[7]Table: 2.2

NO.	SERVISES	COST	BASIS
1.	Registrar & Transfer Agents	Registrar and Agents fees	Number of Unit holders/Certificate holder account Services fee; Number of transactions; Standard outputs and standing charges for maintaining records
2.	Advertiser	Advertiser service fees	Percentage of the total budget of advertisement
3.	Custodian	Custodian fees	Number of transactions in terms of amount
4.	Trustee	Management fees	Average net assets
5.	Advisor	Advisory fees	Average net assets
6.	Underwriters	Underwriters fees	Total offering
7.	Legal Advisor	Legal fees	Actual
8.	Auditors	Audit fees	Actual
9.	Fund officers	Fund officers fees	Actual

2.4 MUTUAL FUNDS AS FINANCIAL INTERMEDIARY:

With the growth of the economy and the capital market in India, the size of investor has also increased rapidly. In fact, small investors in

---

[7] MS-44 Security Analysis and Portfolio Management (IGNOU) study material unit 16 p 32

India have regularly invested in public issues to finance big and small green-field projects of known and unknown promoters. They have been benefited out of such investments in the past. As the stock market crumbled later on and new issues flopped, small investors again started to look for a good opportunity. In this situation, mutual funds provide that they are able to deliver the goods. The concept of mutual funds was conceived to mobilize savings from the people and invest them in a mix of corporate and government securities. The mutual fund operators actively manage the portfolio of schemes and earn income through dividend, interest and capital gains which is eventually passed on to mutual fund investors so mutual funds are financial intermediaries.

Figure: 2.3

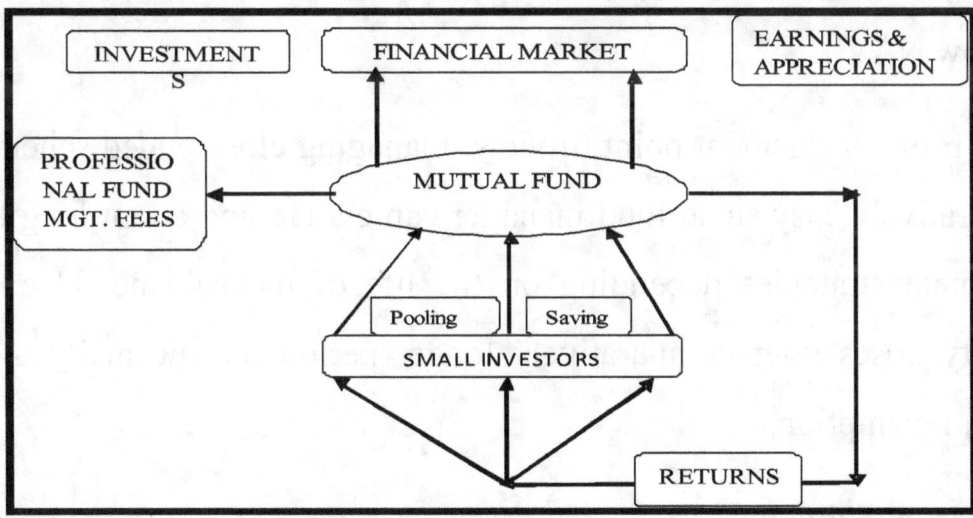

2.5 TYPES OF MUTUAL FUNDS:

Schemes of mutual funds refer to the product they offer to invest. Investors are to choose out of such schemes as per their objective of

No minute to minute fluctuations in rates haunt the investors. In such funds, option to reinvest its dividend is also available.

(2) Close Ended Schemes:

Such schemes have a definite period after which their units are redeemed. Unlike open-ended funds, theses funds have fixed capitalization, i.e. their corpus normally does not change throughout their tenure. While open ended funds are repurchased or sold directly by mutual funds on the basis of NAV, the close ended fund units being quoted on the stock exchanges are traded amongst the investors in the secondary market. Their price is determined on the basis of demand and supply in the market. Their liquidity depends on the efficiency and understanding of the engaged broker. Their price is free to deviate from the NAV, i.e., there is every possibility that market price may be above or below NAV.

From management point of view, managing close ended scheme is comparatively easy since fund manager can evolve and adopt long term investment strategies depending on the life of the scheme. Need for liquidity arises after comparatively longer period, i.e. normally at the time of redemption.

(3) Interval Scheme:

There is a variant of close ended scheme known as Interval Scheme. It is basically a close ended scheme with a peculiar feature that every year for a specified period (interval) it is made open. Prior to and after such specified interval the scheme operates as close ended. During the specified period mutual fund is ready to buy or sell the units directly from or to the investors.

In India as per SEBI (MF) Regulation, every mutual fund is free to launch any or both type of schemes including interval scheme. In the USA, UK and Canada close ended funds are popular as investment companies/trust whereas open ended funds are known as mutual funds. Such distinction is not made in Indian context. In those countries mutual funds were popular than investment companies. Till 1994 mid, in India close ended funds were popular but later on investors' preference for open ended funds forced mutual funds to change their market product.

Return Based Classification:

To meet the diversified needs of investors, the mutual fund schemes are designed accordingly. Basically, all investments are made to earn good returns. Returns expected are in the form of regular dividends or capital appreciation or combination of these two. In the light of this fact, mutual fund schemes can also be classified into three categories on the basis of return.

(1) Income Funds:

For Investors who are more curious for regular returns, Income Funds are floated. Their object is to maximize current income.

Investment is made in fixed income securities like bonds debentures. Such funds distributed periodically the income earned by them. These funds can also be classified into two categories viz. (i) Constant income fund and (ii) Maximum income funds. Obviously the higher the expected return, the higher the potential risk of the investment.

(2) Growth Funds:

These kinds of funds aim at appreciation in the value of the underlying investments through capital appreciation. Such funds invest in growth oriented securities i.e. in shares of companies which can appreciate in long run. Growth funds are also known as **nest eggs** or long haul investments. An investor who selects such fund should be able to assume a higher than normal degree of risk.

(3) Conservative Funds:

The funds with a philosophy of all things to all issue offer document announcing objectives as:

a) To provide a reasonable rate of return.
b) To protect the value of investment and,
c) To achieve capital appreciation consistent with fulfillment of the first two objectives.

Such funds which offer a blend of all these features are known as conservative fund. These funds are also known as middle of the road funds. Such funds divide their portfolio in common stocks and bonds in a way to achieve the desired objectives. Such funds have been most popular and appeal "to the investors who want both growth and income."

Investment-Base Classification:

Mutual Fund may also be classified on the basis of securities in which they invest. Basically, it is renaming the sub-categories of return-base classification.

(1) Equity Fund:

Such funds as the name implies, invest most of their investible funds in equity shares of companies and undertake the risk associated with the investment in equity shares. Such funds are clearly expected to outdo other funds in a rising market, because these have almost all their capital in equity. A special type of equity fund is known as 'Index Fund' or **'Never beat market fund'**. These are known as Index funds since these funds transact only those scrips which are included in any specific index e.g., the scrips which constitute theBSE-30 Sensex or 100 shares National index. The fund consists of a portfolio designed to reflect the composition of some broad based market index and it is done by holding securities in the, same proportion with respect to rupees involved. The value of such index linked funds will go up whenever the market index goes up and conversely, it will come down when the market index comes down. Such fund is not to beat a specific index but is to match that index. These have comparatively lower operating cost.

(2) Bond Fund:

Such funds have their portfolio consisting of bonds, debenture etc. This type of fund is fully secured with a steady income but with little or no chance of capital appreciation. Obviously risk is low in such funds. In this category we may come across the fund called liquid funds which specialize in investing short-term money market instruments. The emphasis is on liquidity and is associated with lower risks and low return.

(3) Balanced Fund:

The funds which have in their portfolio a reasonable mix of equity and bonds are known as balanced funds. Such funds will put more emphasis on equity share investments when the outlook is bright and will tend to switch to debentures when the future is expected to be poor for shares, majority of funds fall in this category, of course, their mix proportion varies.

(4) Fund of funds (FOF):

It is mutual fund scheme that invests in other mutual funds schemes instead of investing in securities. Such schemes are prevalent in international market. These schemes can have different investment patterns and investment strategies as disclosed in offer documents. The investors may invest their fund in those FOF schemes which meet their investment objectives instead of investing in different schemes of a mutual fund and keeping track of their NAVs. Such FOF schemes may invest in other sector specific schemes or those schemes which have more weightage of certain stocks and can exit from those schemes when growth prospects of those sectors are not good. The investors putting their money in one sector specific scheme may not be able to decide when to exit.

Other Classification:

(1) Sectoral Scheme:

Sectoral funds are those, which invest exclusively in a specified industry (sector) of the economy like Pharma fund or IT fund, gold and silver, real estate, or group of industries or various segments such as 'A' Group share or initial public offerings.

(2) Leveraged funds:

Some mutual fund broad base their investible fund by borrowings from the market and then make investments thereby making leverage benefits available to the mutual fund investors. Such funds are known as 'leveraged funds'. It depends on the regulating provisions in a country whether borrowings are allowed or not. Normally leverage funds use short sale, which allows the management of fund to avail the advantage of declining markets in order to realize gains in the portfolio. Leverage funds also use options specifically call options.

(3) Load funds:

A load fund is one that charges a commission for entry or exit. That is, each time you buy or sell Units in the fund, a commission will be payable. Typically entry and exit load range from 1% to 2%. It could be worth paying the load, if the fund has a good performance history.

(4) No load funds:

A load fund is one that does not charge a commission for entry or exit. That is, no commission is payable on purchase or sale of Units in the fund. The advantage of a no load fund is that the entire corpus is put to work.

(5) Tax Savings Schemes:

These schemes offer tax rebate to the investors under specific provisions of the Indian Income tax lows as the Government offers tax incentives for investment in specified avenues. Investments made in Equity Linked savings Schemes (ELSS) and Pension Schemes are allowed as deduction u/s 80 C of the Income Tax Act, 1961.

(6) Index funds: Index funds attempt to replicate the performance of a particular index such as the BSE-50 Sensex or NSE 100 Sensex.

2.6 ADVANTAGES AND DISADVANTAGES OF MUTUAL FUND:

ADVANTAGES:

(1) Professional Management:

The primary advantage of funds is the professional management of your money. Investors purchase funds because they do not have the time or the expertise to manage their own portfolios. A mutual fund is a relatively inexpensive way for a small investor to get a full-time manager to make and monitor investments.

(2) Diversification:

By owning shares in a mutual fund instead of owning individual stocks or bonds, your risk is spread out. The idea behind diversification is to invest in a large number of assets so that a loss in any particular investment is minimized by gains in others. In other words, the more stocks and bonds you own, the less any one of them can hurt you (think about Enron). Large mutual funds typically own hundreds of different stocks in many different industries. It wouldn't be possible for an investor to build this kind of a portfolio with a small amount of money.

(3) Economies of Scale:

Because a mutual fund buys and sells large amounts of securities at a time, its transaction costs are lower than what an individual would pay for securities transactions.

(4) Liquidity:

Just like an individual stock, a mutual fund allows you to request that your shares be converted into cash at any time.

(5) Simplicity:

Buying a mutual fund is easy! Pretty well any bank has its own line of mutual funds, and the minimum investment is small. Most companies also have automatic purchase plans whereby as little as ₹500 can be invested on a monthly basis.

(6) Less Risk:

Investors acquire a diversified portfolio of securities even with a small investment in a Mutual Fund. The risk in a diversified portfolio is lesser than investing in merely 2 or 3 securities.

(7) Choice of Schemes:

Mutual funds provide investors with various schemes with different investment objectives. Investors have the option of investing in a scheme having a correlation between its investment objectives and their own financial goals. These schemes further have different plans/options

(8) Transparency:

Funds provide investors with updated information pertaining to the markets and the schemes. All material facts are disclosed to investors as required by the regulator.

(9) Flexibility:

Investors also benefit from the convenience and flexibility offered by Mutual Funds. Investors can switch their holdings from a debt scheme to an equity scheme and vice-versa. Option of systematic (at regular intervals) investment and withdrawal is also offered to the investors in most open-end schemes.

(10) Safety:

Mutual Fund industry is part of a well-regulated investment environment where the interests of the investors are protected by the regulator. All funds are registered with SEBI and complete transparency is forced.

(11) Tax Advantages:

In so many Mutual fund investment is allowed as deduction under section 80 C of Income tax Act 1961. So investor can get tax benefit by investing in mutual fund.

DISADVANTAGES:

(1) Professional Management:

Many investors debate whether or not the professionals are any better than you or I at picking stocks. Management is by no means infallible, and, even if the fund loses money, the manager still gets paid.

(2) Costs:

Creating, distributing, and running a mutual fund is an expensive proposition. Everything from the manager's salary to the investor's statements cost money. Those expenses are passed on to the investors. Since fees vary widely from fund to fund, failing to pay attention to the fees can have negative long-term consequences. Remember, every rupee spend on fees is a money that has no opportunity to grow over time.

(3) Dilution:

It's possible to have too much diversification. Because funds have small holdings in so many different companies, high returns from a few investments often don't make much difference on the overall return. Dilution is also the result of a successful fund getting too big. When money pours into funds that have had strong success, the manager often has trouble finding a good investment for all the new money.

(4) Taxes:

When a fund manager sells a security, a capital-gains tax is triggered. Investors who are concerned about the impact of taxes need to keep those concerns in mind when investing in mutual funds. Taxes can be mitigated by investing in tax-sensitive funds or by holding non-tax sensitive mutual fund in a tax-deferred account.

(5) Difficulty in Selecting a Suitable Fund Scheme:

Many investors find it difficult to select one option from the plethora of funds/schemes/plans available. For this, they may have to take advice from financial planners in order to invest in the right fund to achieve their objectives.

2.7 VARIOUS INVESTMENT OPTIONS IN MUTUAL FUNDS OFFER:

To cater to different investment needs, Mutual Funds offer various investment options. Some of the important investment options include:

Growth Option: Dividend is not paid-out under a Growth Option and the investor realises only the capital appreciation on the investment (by an   increase   in   NAV).

Dividend Payout Option: Dividends are paid-out to investors under the Dividend Payout Option. However, the NAV of the mutual fund scheme falls   to   the   extent   of   the   dividend   payout.

Dividend Re-investment Option: Here the dividend accrued on mutual funds is automatically re-invested in purchasing additional units in open-ended funds. In most cases mutual funds offer the investor an option of collecting dividends or re-investing the same. **Retirement Pension Option:** Some schemes are linked with retirement pension. Individuals participate in these options for themselves, and corporates participate for their employees. **Insurance Option:** Certain Mutual Funds offer schemes that provide insurance cover to investors as an added benefit. **Systematic Investment Plan (SIP):** Here the investor is given the option of preparing a pre-determined number of post-dated cheques in favour of the fund. The investor is allotted units on a predetermined date specified in the offer document at the applicable NAV. **Systematic Withdrawal Plan (SWP):** As opposed to the Systematic Investment Plan, the Systematic Withdrawal Plan allows the investor the facility to withdraw a pre-determined amount / units from his fund at a pre-determined interval. The investor's units will be redeemed at the applicable NAV as on that day.

2.8 HISTORY AND DEVELOPMENT OF MUTUAL FUND:

Origin of Mutual Fund and growth of Mutual Fund outside India:

Mutual Funds as a concept first originated in the Britain in the 19th century but developed in the U.S. in the late 19th and early 20th century at the principal money centers of North East. These funds were primarily close-ended and used to finance growth in U.S.A. after the Civil War. However, the crash of stock markets in 1929 led to the demise of these close ended funds. In 1940, U.S. had about 68 funds; currently there are several thousands of schemes. More significantly, in the year 1965 there were only 2 to 3% of U.S. households who owned fund share. Nearly one-fourth of all U.S. households invest today in mutual funds. In 1965, U.S. Mutual Fund annual sales were $4.4 billion; in today's term, its monthly sales are twice that level. U.S. Mutual Funds now deal with over five crore shareholder accounts. The secret behind the U.S. success story is that their fund managers have developed mutual funds for all economic conditions and for every investment need. However, not only the U.S. but some other countries of the world also saw the unprecedented growth in this industry. Italy's mutual fund Industry witnessed a growth of 2000%, Japan 600%, U.K.350% and Germany 330%. Countries like Canada, Australia, Mexico and many South American countries too recorded enormous growth during the decade. The mutual fund industry in India was under monopoly of a long time and hence the growth was not very much during the initial period. However, after they are opened up for private sector, the industry has witnessed tremendous growth.

History and growth of Indian mutual fund industry:

In India mutual concept took root only in the 1960s, after a century old history elsewhere in the world. Reacting to the need for a active mobilization of houses hold savings to provide investible resources to industry, the idea of first mutual fund in India, UTI born out the far sighted vision of Shri T.T. Krishnamachari, Finance Minister at that time. UTI in 1964 started with a unit scheme popular as "US-64". Since Unit Trust of India was the result of a special enactment, no other open end mutual fund activities could emerge because of restrictive conditions of Indian Companies Act, 1956. Of course, close end investment companies existed for in house investments as well as portfolio investment for a long time. But their activities were again on restricted scale. The history of Indian Mutual Fund can be divided in for stage viz. (1) 1963-1987, (2) 1987-1993, (3) 1993-2003, (4) Since 2003.

First Stage – 1964-87

Unit Trust of India (UTI) was established on 1963 by an Act of Parliament. It was set up by the Reserve Bank of India and functioned under the Regulatory and administrative control of the Reserve Bank of India. In 1978 UTI was de-linked from the RBI and the Industrial Development Bank of India (IDBI) took over the regulatory and administrative control in place of RBI. The first scheme launched by UTI was Unit Scheme 1964. At the end of June, 1987 total ₹4563 crores of assets under management. Major share was of UTI. In 1987 the monopoly of UTI came to an end when Government of India by amending Banking Regulation Act enabled commercial banks in public sector to set up mutual fund as their subsidiaries. First of all State Bank of India got a nod from RBI. Next to follow was Canara Bank. It was Abid Hussion Committee's unequivocal support to the concept that could be accepted as something of a landmark. It called for a greater number of mutual fund players. LIC and GIC also entered in field of mutual funds.

Second Stage – 1987-1993 (Entry of Public Sector Funds):

1987 marked the entry of non- UTI, public sector mutual funds set up by public sector banks and Life Insurance Corporation of India (LIC) and General Insurance Corporation of India (GIC). SBI Mutual Fund was the first non- UTI Mutual Fund established in June 1987 followed by Canbank Mutual Fund (Dec 87), Punjab National Bank Mutual Fund (Aug 89), Indian Bank Mutual Fund (Nov 89), Bank of India (Jun 90), Bank of Baroda Mutual Fund (Oct 92). LIC established its mutual fund in June 1989 while GIC had set up its mutual fund in December 1990.

In pre 1992 period, Indian mutual funds had certain peculiarities. These are:

- Mutual funds in our country till this period were public sector banks and financial institutions.

- Another distinguishing feature was that majority of mutual fund have been floated by commercial banks and financial institutions which gave the impression in the minds of investors that responsibility of funds lies with the respective banks thus their investment is secured.

- One feature which distinguished mutual funds in India from their counterparts in Europe were that the latter normally do not have an in built promise of minimum return. The experience of UTI showed that its schemes with assured returns had tremendous success.

- Disclosure practices of mutual funds were far away from international standards despite the specific provisions in the regulatory framework.

- One of the important features of mutual fund success in raising respectable quantum of fund was the associated tax concessions.

- The launching of mutual funds by commercial banks during 1986-87 was in the peculiar circumstances of the absence of any regulatory framework for conduct of the affairs.

At the end of 1993, the mutual fund industry had assets under management of ₹47,004 crores.

Third Stage– 1993-2003 (Entry of Private Sector Funds)

With the entry of private sector funds in 1993, a new era started in the Indian mutual fund industry, giving the Indian investors a wider choice of fund families. Also, 1993 was the year in which the first Mutual Fund Regulations came into being, under which all mutual funds, except UTI were to be registered and governed. The erstwhile

Kothari Pioneer (now merged with Franklin Templeton) was the first private sector mutual fund registered in July 1993.

The 1993 SEBI (Mutual Fund) Regulations were substituted by a more comprehensive and revised Mutual Fund Regulations in 1996. The industry now functions under the SEBI (Mutual Fund) Regulations 1996.

The number of mutual fund houses went on increasing, with many foreign mutual funds setting up funds in India and also the industry has witnessed several mergers and acquisitions. As at the end of January 2003, there were 33 mutual funds with total assets of ₹1,21,805 crores. The Unit Trust of India with ₹44,541 crores of assets under management was way ahead of other mutual funds.

Fourth Stage – since February 2003

In February 2003, following the repeal of the Unit Trust of India Act 1963 UTI was bifurcated into two separate entities. One is the Specified Undertaking of the Unit Trust of India with assets under management of Rs.29,835 crores as at the end of January 2003, representing broadly, the assets of US 64 scheme, assured return and certain other schemes. The Specified Undertaking of Unit Trust of India, functioning under an administrator and under the rules framed by Government of India and does not come under the purview of the Mutual Fund Regulations. The 1993 SEBI (Mutual Fund) Regulations were substituted by a more comprehensive and revised Mutual Fund Regulations in 1996. The industry now functions under the SEBI (Mutual Fund) Regulations 1996.The second is the UTI Mutual Fund, sponsored by SBI, PNB, BOB and LIC. It is registered with SEBI and functions under the Mutual Fund Regulations. With the bifurcation of the erstwhile UTI which had in March 2000 more than ₹76,000 crores of assets under management and with the setting up of a UTI Mutual Fund, conforming to the SEBI Mutual Fund Regulations, and with recent mergers taking place among different private sector funds, the mutual fund industry has entered its current phase of consolidation and growth. The number of mutual fund houses went on increasing, with many foreign mutual funds setting up funds in India and also the industry has witnessed several mergers and acquisitions. As at the end of March 2011 total number of mutual fund registered with SEBI 49 and total assets under management was ₹592250 crore.

The graph indicates the growth of assets over the years.

Graph 2.1

8

---

[8] http://www.amfiindia.com/showhtml.aspx?page=mfindustry

2.9 LIST OF REGISTERED MUTUAL FUND IN INDIA WITH SEBI:

Table: 2.3

No.	NAME AND ADDRESSES	Registration No.	Registration Date
1.	Taurus Mutual Fund Ground Floor, AML Centre-1, 8 Mahal Industrial Estate, Mahakali Caves Road Andheri (E), Mumbai – 400093 Tel: 022- 66242700, Fax: 022-66242722 Website: www.taurusmutualfund.com Email: info@taurusmutualfund.com	MF/002/93/	21.9.1993
2.	ICICI Prudential Mutual Fund 2nd Floor, 302, Block B-2, Nirlon Knowledge Park, Western Express Highway, Mumbai - 400063. Tel No. +9122 42090573 **Registered Office :** 12th Floor, Narain Manzil, 23, Barakhamba Road, New Delhi – 110 001 WEB : www.pruicici.com	MF/003/93/ 6	13.10.1993
3.	Canara Robeco Mutual Fund Construction House, 4th Floor, 5, Walchand Hirachand Marg, Ballard Estate, Mumbai 400 001. Tel : 6658 5000 to 5010, Fax 6658 5011 to 5013 WEB : www.canararobeco.com Email : crmf@canararobeco.com	MF/004/93/ 4	19.10.1993
4.	Morgan Stanley Mutual Fund	MF/005/93/	5.11.1993

	19th Floor, One Indiabulls Centre, Tower 2, Jupiter Mils Compound, 841, Senapati Bapat Marg, Elphinstone Road, Mumbai - 400 013. TEL : 61181000, FAX : 61181027 WEB : www.morganstanley.com/indiamf	1	
5.	CRB Mutual Fund (Suspended) Daruwala Mansion, 3rd Floor, 90 Chandanwadi Cross Lane, Mumbai 400 020. TEL : 2072719/20, FAX : 2096433	MF/008/93/5	17.12.1993
6.	SBI Mutual Fund 191, Maker Towers "E", Cuffe Parade Mumbai 400005 TEL : 22180221-25,27, FAX : 22189663 WEB : www.sbimf.com	MF/009/93/3	23.12.1993
7.	LIC Nomura Mutual Fund Industrial Assurance Bldg., 4th Floor, Opp Churchgate Stn., Mumbai 400 020. TEL : 22851661/22851663, FAX : 22040039 WEB : www.licmutual.com	MF/012/94/5	9.5.1994
8.	JM Financial Mutual Fund 502, 5th Floor, 'A' Wing, Laxmi Towers, Bandra Kurla Complex, Mumbai - 400051 TEL : 39877777, FAX : 26528377-78 WEB : www.JMFinancialmf.com Email : mktg@jmmutual.com	MF/015/94/8	15.9.1994
9.	Shriram Mutual Fund 106, Shiv Chambers, 1stFloor, 'B'	MF/017/94/4	21.11.1994

	Wing Sector - 11, C.B.D.Belapur, Navi Mumbai 400 614. TEL : 7901447/8, FAX : 7901449 Email: srmf@roltanet.com		
10.	Baroda Pioneer Mutual Fund 501, Titanium, 5th floor, Western Express Highway, Goregaon (E), Mumbai 400 063. TEL : 307410000, 42197999, FAX :30741001 WEB : www.barodapioneer.in Email : info@barodapioneer.in	MF/018/94/ 2	21.11.1994
11.	Principal Mutual Fund Exchange Plaza, 2nd Floor, B Wing, NSE Building, Bandra Kurla Complex, Bandra(East) Mumbai 400051. TEL : 67720555, FAX : 2204 4990 Toll Free No: 1800225600 WEB : www.principalindia.com Email : customer@principalindia.com	MF/019/94/ 0	13.12.1994
12.	Birla Sunlife Mutual Fund One India Bulls Centre, Tower-1, 17th Floor, Jupiter Mills Compound, 841, Senapati Bapat Marg, Elphinstone Road, Mumbai- 400001 TEL : 43568000, FAX : 43568110/8111 WEB : www.birlasunlife.com	MF/020/94/ 8	23.12.1994
13.	Alliance Capital Mutual Fund, Address for correspondence C/o. AZB & Partners Advocates & Solicitors, Express Towers – 23rd Floor, Nariman Point, Mumbai – 400 021	MF/021/95/ 3	30.12.1994

14.	Tata Mutual Fund, Mafatlal Center, 9th Floor, Nariman Point, Mumbai 400 021. TEL : 66578282, FAX : 22613782 WEB : www.tatamutualfund.com Email kiran@tataamc.com	MF/023/95/9	30.6.1995
15.	Reliance Mutual Fund One India Bulls Centre, Tower 1, 11th 7 12th Floor, Jupiter Mills Compound, 841 Senapati Bapat Marg, Elphinstone Road, Mumbai 400 001. TEL : 30287168, FAX : 30414885 WEB: www.reliancemutual.com Email:customer_care@reliancemutual.com	MF/022/95/1	30.6.1995
16.	Franklin Templeton Mutual Fund Level 4, Wockhardt Towers, Bandra Kurla Complex, Bandra (East), Mumbai – 400 051 TEL : 6751 9100, FAX : 6649 0622 WEB : www.templetonindia.com	MF/026/96/8	19.2.1996
17.	Escorts Mutual Fund, 11, Scindia House, Connaught Circus, New Delhi 110 001. TEL : 011-3321654 / 5177 / 3319991 / 3351343, FAX : 011-23761495, 23325177 WEB: www.escortsmutual.com Email : help@escortsmutual.com TEL : 30947097, 24218162	MF/028/96/4	3.7.1996
18.	Sahara Mutual Fund, 9th Floor, 97-98, Atlanta Building Nariman Point, Mumbai – 400 021	MF/030/96/0	1.10.1996

	Tel : 22-6752 0121 – 27, Fax : 66547855 WEB : www.saharamutual.com Email: saharamutual@saharamutual.com		
19.	L&T Mutual Fund 309, Trade Centre, 3rd Floor, Bandra Kurla Complex, Bandra (East), Mumbai - 400 051. TEL : 66574000, FAX : 66574004 WEB : www.lntmf.com E-mail: ltmf@lntmf.com	MF/035/97/9	3.1.1997
20.	Sundaram Mutual Fund, 46, Whites Road, Royapettah, Chennai 600 014. TEL : 044-28543362/28543367, FAX : 044-28543156	MF/034/97/2	3.1.1997
21.	DSP BlackRock Mutual Fund, Mafatlal Centre, 10th Floor, Nariman Point, Mumbai 400 021. TEL : 66578000, FAX: 66578181 WEB : www.dspblackrock.com Email : service@dspblackrock.com Toll Free No: 1800 345 4499	MF/036/97/7	30.1.1997
22.	Kotak Mahindra Mutual Fund, Kotak Towers, 6th Floor, Bldg. No. 21, Infinity Park, Gen. A. K. Vaidya Marg, Malad (E), Mumbai – 400 097 TEL : 66384444, FAX : 66384455 WEB : www.kotakmutual.com	MF/038/98/1	23.6.1998
23.	ING Mutual Fund, Unit No. 101, 601/606, 6th Floor, "Windsor", Off. C.S.T. Road, Vidyanagari Marg,	MF/040/99/5	11.2.1999

	Kalina, Santacruz (East), Mumbai – 400 098 TEL : 022-39827999, Toll Free : 18004255433 FAX : 022-26500248, Email : information@in.ing.com, WEB : www.ingim.co.in		
24.	KJMC Mutual Fund, 168, Atlanta, 16th Floor, Nariman Point Mumbai 400 021 TEL : 22885201/22832350, FAX : 22852892 Email : kjmcmutual@kjmcmutual.com	MF/041/99/4	28.4.1999
25.	IDFC Mutual Fund, One IndiaBulls Centre, 841, Jupiter Mills Compound, Senapati Bapat Marg, Elphinstone Road (West), Mumbai – 400 013. TEL : 22621111, FAX : 22693365 Email : investor@idfcmf.com WEB : www.idfcmf.com	MF/042/00/3	13.3.2000
26.	ICICI Securities Fund, ICICI Towers, 7th Floor, North Block, Bandra-Kurla Complex, Mumbai 400 051. TEL : 6531414 / 6538988 (D), FAX : 6531063 / 6531178	MF/043/00/3	28.3.2000
27.	HDFC Mutual Fund, Ramon House, 3rd Floor, 169, Backbay Reclamation, Churchgate, Mumbai 400 020., TEL : 22029111 FAX: 22028862, WEB :	MF/044/00/6	30.6.2000

	www.hdfcfund.com		
28.	HSBC Mutual Fund, 314 D N Road, Fort, Mumbai 400 001. TEL : 66145000, FAX: 40029600 Email : hsbcmf@hsbc.co.in	MF/046/02/5	27.5.2002
29.	Deutsche Mutual Fund 2nd Floor, 222, Kodak House, Dr. D. N. Road, Mumbai 400 001. TEL : 22072211, FAX : 22074411 WEB : http://www.deutschemutual.com Email : deutsche.mutual@db.com	MF/047/02/10	28.10.2002
30.	UTI Mutual Fund UTI Towers, 'Gn' Block, Bandra-Kurla Complex, Bandra (East), Mumbai 400 051 TEL : 56786666, FAX : 56786578 WEB : www.utimf.com	MF/048/03/1	14.01.2003
31.	BNP Paribas Mutual Fund 1 North Avenue, Maker Maxity Bandra Kurla Complex, Mumbai-400 051 Tel- 91 (22) 3370 4000, Fax- 91 (22) 3370 4294 WEB : www.bnpparibasmf.in Email: customercare@bnpparibasmf.in	MF/049/04/01	27.05.2004
32.	Fidelity Mutual Fund 6th floor, Mafatlal Centre, Nariman Point, Mumbai 400 021 TEL: Toll Free number 1-600-121262, Gurgaon : +91 (0124) 509 2104 (Investor Relations Officer's number) Mumbai : + 91 (022) 5655 4000, FAX:	MF/050/05/01	17.02.2005

	Gurgaon : +91 (0124) 509 2100 Mumbai: +91 (022) 5655 4200 Email: investor.line@fidelity.co.in WEB : www.fidelity.co.in		
33.	Quantum Mutual Fund, 505, 5th Floor, Regent Chambers, Nariman Point, Mumbai – 400021 TEL : 22830322, FAX : 22854318 WEB : www.quantumamc.com	MF/051/05/02	02.12.2005
34.	Religare Mutual Fund 3rd Floor, GYS Infinity, Paranjpe "B" Scheme, Subhash Road, Vile Parle (East), Mumbai – 400 057. TEL : 67310000, FAX : 28371565	MF/052/06/01	24.07.2006
35.	JP Morgan Mutual Fund J.P. Morgan Towers, Off C.S.T. Road, Kalina, Santacruz – East. Mumbai 400 098 TEL : 6157 3000, FAX : 6157 4170 WEB : www.jpmorganmf.com Email : india.investors@jpmorgan.com	MF/053/07/01	08.02.2007
36.	AIG Global Investment Group Mutual Fund FCH House, Ground Floor Peninsula Corporate Park Ganpatrao Kadam Marg, Lower Parel Mumbai – 400 013 FAX: 24255100	MF/054/07/02	09.02.2007
37.	Mirae Asset Mutual Fund Unit 606, 6th Floor, Windsor, Off CST Road, Kalina, Santacruz (E), MUMBAI 400 098 TEL : 67800300, FAX : 6725 3942 / 45	MF/055/07/03	30.11.2007

	Email : customercare@miraeassetmf.co.in WEB : www.miraeassetmf.co.in		
38.	Bharti AXA Mutual Fund 51, 5th Floor, Kalpataru Synergy, East Wing, Vakola, Santacruz (E), Mumbai 400 055. TEL : 40479000, FAX : 40479001 Web : www.bhartiaxa-im.com Email: info@bhartiaxa-im.com	MF/056/08/01	31.03.2008
39.	Edelweiss Mutual Fund 14th Floor, Express Towers, Nariman Point, Mumbai – 400 021 TEL : 022-22864400, FAX : 022-4097 9970 Email: investor.amc@edelcap.com Website: www.edelweissmf.com	MF/057/08/02	30.04.2008
40.	Goldman Sachs Mutual Fund Rational House, Appasaheb Marathe Marg, Prabhadevi, Mumbai 400025 TEL : 66169000, FAX : 66279240 Email: gsamindia@gs.com, WEB: www.gsam.in	MF/058/08/03	26.08.2008
41.	Daiwa Mutual Fund, 5th Floor, Harchandrai House, 81, Maharshi Karve Road, Marine Lines, Mumbai – 400 002 TEL : 022-66142900, FAX : 022-66100148 WEB : www.daiwa.in	MF/060/09/01	10.02.2009
42.	Axis Mutual Fund, 1st Floor, Axis House, Bombay Dyeing Mills Compound,	MF/061/09/01	04.09.2009

	Pandurang Budhkar Marg, Worli, Mumbai 400025 TEL : 39403300, FAX : 22040130 WEB : www.axismf.com, www.axismutual.com Email customerservice@axismf.com Toll Free No : 1800 3000 3300		
43.	Peerless Mutual Fund Peerless Mansion, 1 Chowringhee Square, Kolkata-700069 TEL : 033-22435496, FAX : 033-22435339 Mumbai office: Ground 03, Churchgate Chambers, Premises Co-operative Housing Society Ltd, Plot - 05, Sir. Vithaldas Thackersay Marg, Next to American Centre, Mumbai - 400 020 Email: pfmc@peerless.co.in WEB : www.peerlessmf.co.in	MF/062/09/ 03	04.12.2009
44.	Motilal Oswal Mutual Fund 81/82, 8th Floor, Bajaj Bhawan, Nariman Point, Mumbai 400 021 Tel: 39804200 Web: www.motilaloswal.com/assetmanagem ent	MF/063/09/ 04	29.12.2009
45.	IDBI Mutual Fund 5th Floor, Mafatlal Centre, Nariman Point, Mumbai 400 021. Tel.: 66442800, Fax: 66442801	MF/064/10/ 01	29.3.2010

	E-mail: Krishnamurthy.vijayan@idbimutual.co .in www.idbimutual.co.in		
46.	Pramerica Mutual Fund Nirlon House, 2nd Floor, Dr. Annie Besant Road, Worli, Mumbai- 400025 TEL: 022- 61593000, FAX: 022-61593100	MF/065/10/02	13.5.2010
47.	IIFL Mutual Fund IIFL Centre, 3rd Floor Annex, Kamala City, Senapati Bapat Marg, Lower Parel, Mumbai-400013 Tel : 42499000, Fax : 40609049 Web: indiainfoline.com	MF/067/11/2	23.3.2011
48.	Indiabulls Mutual Fund One Indiabulls Centre, Tower 2, Basement, Jupiter Mills, Fitwala Road, Near Sai Mandir, Opposite Deepak Talkies, Elphinstone Road, Mumbai – 400013 Tel: 30439414, Fax: 39805325	MF/068/11/3	24.3.2011
49.	Union KBC Mutual Fund 7th Floor, Piramal Tower, Peninsula Corporate Park, Ganpatrao Kadam Marg, Lower Parel (West) Mumbai – 400013 Tel: 2483 3300, Fax: 2483 3401 Web: www.unionkbc.com	MF/066/11/1	23.3.2011

Source: http://www.sebi.gov.in/investor/mfadd.pdf

1.1 PURPOSE OF DISSERTATION AND SELECTION OF TOPIC:

As a part of curriculum of M. Phil, I have to prepare dissertation on one of the subject specified by Hemchandracharya North Gujarat University Patan. I selected the topic **"A STUDY ON AWARENESS AND BEHAVIOR OF INDIVIDUAL INVESTORS TOWARDS MUTUAL FUND"** with reference to Mehsana and Patan region.

As we probably know, mutual funds have become extremely popular over the last 15 years among individual investor in India. Till 1986, the Unit Trust of India was the only mutual fund in India. Since then public sector banks and insurance companies have been allowed to set up subsidiaries to undertake mutual fund business. So State bank of India, Canara Bank, LIC, GIC, and few other public sector banks entered the mutual fund industry. In 1992, the mutual fund industry was opened to the private sector and a number of private sector mutual funds such as Birla Mutual Fund, DSP Merill Lynch Mutual fund, HDFC Mutual Fund, IDBI Principal Mutual Fund, Tata Mutual Fund, Kotak Mahindra Mutual Fund etc. are entered in Indian mutual fund industry. Day by day such mutual fund offers different type of scheme to the individual investors at present total 49 registered mutual funds with SEBI and managing nearly 1000 schemes.

As a M. Phil student I studied the growth and development of mutual fund industries in India in depth. I also studied the behavior and awareness of individual investors by collecting information personally from investors. In this study I had trying to know that what the individual investor think about investment in mutual fund, whether mutual fund satisfied the investors need and expectation. I did this work in Mehsana and Patan region urban area only. I was trying to my subject at the level best.

1.2 OBJECTIVES OF THE STUDY:

MAIN OBJECTIVES:

The main objective of this study is to understand and analyze the awareness and behavior of individual investors toward mutual funds through an individual investor's survey in Mehsana and Patan region.

SUB OBJECTIVE:

Following aspects/ points will be analyzed during the study:-

- Study of awareness and behavior of individual investors towards mutual fund

- Study of behavior of individual investors towards various investment alternatives like bank deposits, bonds, stock, real assets etc.

- To assess the savings objectives among individual investors.

- To identify the preferred savings avenue among individual investors.

- To understand the preferential feature in the savings instrument among individual investors.

- To assess Mutual fund conceptual awareness among present investors.

- To assess the fund/ scheme preference of investors.

- To evaluate fund qualities that would affect the selection of Mutual funds.

- To perceive the preferred communication mode of investors.

- To understand the fund sponsor qualities influencing the selection of MFs/Schemes.

- To identify the information sources influencing the scheme selection decision of investors.

- To identify the most popular Mutual Funds among individual investors.

- To assess the influence of personal variables on the MF conceptual awareness level of individual investors.

- To evaluate investor related services that would affect the selection of Mutual funds.

- To establish a relationship between types of investors and MF qualities that influence MF/Scheme selection

1.3 MEANING OF INDIVIDUAL INVESTORS AND REASONS FOR THEIR INVESTMENT:

An individual are those who purchase small amounts of securities for his/herself, as opposed to an institutional investors, also called retail investors or small investors

An individual who are commits his or her money to investment products with the expectation of financial return. Generally, the primary concern of investors is to minimize risk while maximizing return, as opposed to a speculator, who is willing to accept a higher level of risk in the hopes of collecting higher-than –average profits.